The Memory Inferno: My secret journey to power

Pele Burn

ISBN-13:
978-1975863302

ISBN-10:
1975863305

Dedicated to Pele

The fire goddess

May she burn your shield and reveal your light

CONTENTS

1 PELE

My real name is not Pele. Pele is the legendary fire goddess who gave me the inspiration for this book. She guards the volcano in Kilauea, Big Island, Hawaii. It was there I created my Memory Inferno. I followed my bad feelings back to their roots and ripped them out like the core of a neglected wart which had been allowed to live in my skin unattended to. I burned them in the volcano and pledged to live a life of joy, passion and playfulness.

I am happy now. I am also a young millionaire, I have a very successful legal career, I am very happily married and I am blessed with good health. I "literally" love everything about my life.

I came here from darkness. Almost a decade ago, I tried with intent and a sharp knife, to kill myself.

I now know that I was living a life that I was responsible for. I was feeling bad feelings that I created. I did not understand that then. I thought that life happened to me and that I was destined for those feelings. I was so very wrong.

We can all choose to be happy, whatever we feel we are now. I had a journey from poverty, anorexia and bulimia, depression and other anxiety disorders, through a suicide attempt, to a healthy, wealthy and happy me.

In many cases of people achieving wealth and fame, there is a negative emotion acting as a driving force, causing a craving feeling for wealth and attention. An underlying feeling of desperation, poverty, insecurity, or lack of respect from other people. A feeling in the depths of the soul of worthlessness, so we look outside for validation that we are worth something.

Wealth and attention feel good. Excitement feels good. Achievements feel good. The feelings generated by these things can mask a deep feeling of sadness. There are certain professions which attract depressed individuals with a talent. Comedians, ironically, are usually lonely and sad when are not performing. What drives them to succeed is a feeling of deep sadness and loneliness that they can only forget by the feeling of recognition and achievement when an audience laughs at their performance. Actors, supermodels, singer-songwriters, sports stars, are very frequently driven by a need for the validation of millions of people loving their work, or their body. Without millions of fans, they feel worthless. The mass irresponsible criticism that comes with fame reinforces their feelings of worthlessness. Monstrous individuals in positions of power reinforce their feelings of worthlessness.

People who feel worthless are all around us every day, whatever we are doing. According to www.healthresearchfunding.org, one million people actually succeed in committing suicide every year. Some of them are in the news: Superstars with destructive alcohol and drug habits; Self-made millionaires who go bankrupt; Billionaire fraudsters.

Fame and money is not what killed them. It does not make their deaths any less tragic, but fame and money are not the enemy. If you believe that money is the enemy, you are no doubt poor, and if you have money but you hate it, you will go bankrupt without even trying.

The enemy is the root of the bad feelings. If we do not address it and instead we only mask bad feelings, they come back again. Wealth, achievements and attention only act as a temporary plaster if they are driven by the desperate need to mask a bad feeling. If you are sad, you can practice the law of attraction and imagine anything you want into your life, but it will all be a mask if you do not figure out what or who made you feel bad.

The bad feelings have to be dumped. For me that meant digging them out and metaphorically burning them in dramatic recognition of the fact that I do not need them and they have no power over me. Those feelings are ugly and painful, but they had to be found and destroyed.

If you are not happy, you can turn your life around. Whatever you want is yours. If you think anyone else is responsible for how you feel, then I am telling you that you are as wrong as I was.

Right now, and in any moment, you are responsible for how you feel. You are responsible for feeling fantastic, or for feeling worthless, whichever you choose.

I believe that your destiny is to feel great. You personally. I believe that if you are feeling bad you are wrong to do so. I do not tell you this lightly. I know what it is like to feel worthless and helpless.

If you want to go from zero to being your very own hero, read on. But I can tell you that if you do not reflect on you, then you will get next to nothing out of this book. You may think I tell some interesting stories about my own experiences, but the point of me writing this is that I believe

I can help you to help yourself. You get what you focus on. I have an extremely successful career doing something entirely different. I focused on that like a drowning man on the prospect of air for two decades. Then I realized I had failed to focus on me in all that time. That is when I discovered Pele. Pele set my life on fire and created an awesome version of me. The answers are all inside you. Everything you experience is a reflection of how you are feeling on the inside. Your feelings flow from your thoughts. Stop the bad thoughts, stop the bad feelings, make way for great ones.

Pele's work is a practice. Like anything, the more you practice the better the results you get. As you read this book, I suggest you have a note pad and pen to hand. Your note pad is your very own "Memory Inferno".

If you do the work I suggest then it will contain the thoughts that have been creating your very own hell. All the bad feelings you have ever felt. Things have to get worse before they can get better. Acknowledging what you have been creating, probably for years, will set you free. Your Memory Inferno will also be the bonfire that will set you alight.

I practiced the Memory Inferno and I will tell you what I found as we go along. It is important that you do not judge what you learn about your current position. You may be surprised or shocked about what you discover about your feelings for yourself and the patterns you have created. You may not want to believe that you create your own reality because it is easier to blame other people or things. But the truth is that the only thing you can control is your own thoughts and feelings, once you learn to do that everything becomes easy.

You may see deep pain on the page. Whatever comes out, it is a beautiful release. In releasing the old patterns we make emotional space which is naturally filled with love and gives us the power to create.

Dante's Inferno was apparently autobiographical in that it starts with an expression of his own midlife crisis as hell. Macabre as it may be to read (at least I find it so…) it is beautiful. Edvard Munch's most famous painting "The Scream" was said by him to be a study of his own tortured soul. Amy Winehouse's Back to Black was a window to the emotions from her childhood heartbreak that she never broke free from. She repeated their destruction with misapprehended love and drugs. There is an obvious lesson that if we do not acknowledge the root cause of our bad emotions and destroy it, it has the potential to destroy us instead: Our feelings, our relationships, our finances, our health, and everything that happens in our lives every day. It also drives people to suicide.

You may produce something beautiful in this process, it may be too painful for you to look at, you can literally burn it if so (in a safe place!) when your done letting it out. Just let it out, and do not judge it. As soon as you recognize the emotion it loses its power over you and leaves you free to love you instead. To attract wonderful things and events in to your life, and wonderful people who love you too.

Devoting time to doing this work is already a commitment to loving yourself. If you intend to commit to this, you already love yourself.

This work is about becoming the real you. The real you feels like a wonderful perfect being regardless of what you achieve or what you own. You feel loved and you are. When you feel like you are supposed to, everything in your physical world will be a reflection of that.

It is not about dropping material possessions that make you excited or not attracting them, it is actually quite the opposite. It is about being the most powerful magnet you can be. If the magnet is covered in mud (or a more pungent substance) it will not be effective. This is about cleaning the magnet.

Read the following quote out aloud. Repeat this until you actually believe it and feel it. Then write it in your Memory Inferno:

"Right now, I love myself. The work I do in this book makes me love myself more and more all the time."

Carry your Memory Inferno around with you all the time in the first week. Each time you think, feel or say anything which is not positive, you have to take the time aside to write it in the Memory Inferno. If you cannot carry a physical pad, you can text yourself or email yourself instead. What is important is that you write bad feelings in the past tense because as soon as you do that, the feeling is gone, it no longer controls you or your thoughts or actions. These may seem insignificant, like having a knee jerk aggressive reaction to someone else's driving, or someone at work who seems to be in your way, someone who insults you. It may be anger, frustration, boredom. Maybe you take feedback at work or from friends and family as personal criticism when it was intended to be constructive.

If you can, carry a small pad around with you, or you can do this at home in the evening, split the page into two columns, and write bad thoughts in the past tense on the left and good thoughts in the present tense) in the right hand column. I will explain in more detail how this works as we go along. I also explain what I found and what was in my columns. Do not judge the thoughts, mine or yours! For as long as we are judging things we are holding on to them. We are giving them our precious energy and focus instead of letting them go.

One of my favourite zen parables is the two monks traveling together. At one point, they came to a river with a strong current. As the monks were preparing to cross the river, they saw a very young and beautiful woman also attempting to cross. The young woman asked if they could help her cross to the other side. The two monks glanced at one another because they had taken vows not to touch a woman. One of them picked up the woman, carried her across the river, placed her gently on the other side, and carried on his journey. The other monk was so angry he could not speak for hours. They continued on their journey and after several hours of silent anger, he finally blurted out to the other monk "how can you justify carrying that woman, we are not allowed to touch women".

The response he got was, "Brother, I set her down on the other side of the river, why are you still carrying her?"

2 PELE'S WORK

The aim of this process is to get to a place where you can focus on being the awesome version of you that you are meant to be. Focus on being your authentic self, and you will be awesome. You do not need external validation of how great you are. You will get it anyway, because life is a reflection of your feelings and thoughts. It truly is. The more you love you, the more the rest of the world will love you. The point though, is to love you.

Doing the work is about letting go of the things you have been focusing on instead of loving yourself. Finding all the reasons why you have been feeling bad, or not feeling much at all. It is about finding where you are right now. It is important not to judge this. Judging yourself or anyone else is a complete waste of energy, and guess what, it makes you feel bad. So do not judge.

I have structured this book in accordance with the following process, which you need to do in every single area of your life, all of the time.

You will achieve results you never even dreamed were possible with this work. Massive life changing events will happen and mini miracles will occur all around you every day. You will begin to feel blessed and loved like never before.

Step One

Firstly, you need to notice what you are thinking and feeling in every moment of every single day. You are literally wasting your life in the moments you are either not thinking and feeling, or you are thinking bad thoughts and feeling bad. It is time to notice where you are now. What are you feeling?

In particular, you need to notice when you are re-living the past, in your mind and your emotions. I was in complete denial when I asked myself to do this the first time. I thought I was so clever and that I had analysed and discussed my objectively (and apparently quite stereotypical) awful childhood, so frequently that I thought there was no way I was not over it. My mind said "Look around me dude, I am awesome!" I also thought had great relationships with all those people from my childhood so I must have been over it. I was so wrong. The mind and body and soul get mapped out when we are children and we subconsciously follow that map in everything, even when we consciously think we are doing something different. I thought I had escaped my childhood in my early twenties, by which time I had a great job, a degree, several professional qualifications and awards, great friends and a nice house. Then one night, I felt the same worthless feeling I had felt before as a child. The plasters fell off.

It is only when you can recognise what you are doing that you can let it go and consciously dissolve it in love.

In this, you have to be honest with yourself, or it is pointless. I repeat, do not judge what goes in your Memory Inferno, you are where you are. You have to notice the start line, that is all. Beyond noticing it, we do not give it any attention, we will be gone from there in a moment. Do you feel angry sometimes? Do you ever meet up with friends or your other half and spend the whole of that valuable time just letting of steam about something or someone? Do you sit at a desk at work doing something mind numbingly boring, in a daze so that time goes by and you do not know what you were thinking about, if anything? Do you react to things instead of instigating them? Do you do things just to "pass time" instead of because you want to? Do you go shopping and not remember who you saw or spoke to during that time? Do you get so drunk you cannot even remember a whole evening (or you try not to)? When you are listening to a friend tell you a story about something, are you projecting your own feelings on to the situation, or listening to the information they are telling you and wondering what they are feeling? How do you feel when you talk to people during the day? Do you ever feel "harassed" by people or events? Do you feel frustrated by tiny obstacles? Do certain things make you panic? Do you obsess over small things or projects or goals you set yourself?

Step Two

Secondly, you need to appreciate just how powerful your thoughts are. Thoughts are feelings and vice versa. Feelings draw your reality to you. Thoughts are real things, it is a scientific fact. There are many critics of the law of attraction, but there are also many accomplished scientists who conclude that everything in the world is made of quantum particles. There is a wonderful book called "Reality is not what it seems, the Journey to Quantum Gravity" by Carlo Rovelli, which describes the scientific discoveries and theories from the time of Democritus to Einstein's theory of special relativity and modern day physics. Modern day physicists agree with Einstein on his theory of special relativity. Thoughts and feelings are energy, which is matter and which attracts other like matter. The energy which you send out in to the world attracts other energy which is the same. It is that scientific.

Look for proof of this in the first few days of doing the work. Look for signs. Notice what appears around you that you were focusing on. The universe gives you signs all the time, there is no such thing as a coincidence. These will be good or bad, depending on whatever you chose to focus on.

I had a day at work when I felt that my colleagues were giving me "crap to clear up", and I became angry and voiced this in my head and out loud. That evening I returned home from work to find a grown man physically doing a crap outside my house. Of course I cleared it up, I caused it with my thoughts. I wish for you good thoughts and good reflections from the universe! Whatever you imagine and feel, will appear in your life.

There is an exact science to imagining and manifesting your reality. The modern day spiritual leaders and scientists agree on this. Maharishi Mahesh Yogi's book "Science of Being and Art of Living: Transcendental meditation" appears to be explaining what scientists describe as "spacetime" or fields. It is accessed by quietening the mind and getting rid of our thoughts and feelings, detaching yourself from your mind. When we quieten the mind we access infinite possibilities. Deepak Chopra describes it as "the field of pure potentiality" and "the gap". It is here we should plant our intentions.

Werner Heisenburg realized that electrons are always present, there is no such thing as space, it is just that matter only appears when it interacts with other matter. So electrons only appear when they collide with other matter. There is no space, everything is matter. When an electron is not colliding with other matter, in that moment it is pure possibility. This is where thoughts turn to things faster than the speed of light.

Bring this knowledge with you as you do the work. If you do not know it already, or you cannot bring yourself to believe it, read at least one book on it. If you think nothing, you experience nothing. If you focus on nothing, you get nothing back. If you focus on bad things, you give them energy and life, your life that you should be spending feeling good instead. So give them no energy. Give your energy only to things you love. If you do not love yourself right now, make this the focus. You are going to love you.

I would highly recommend meditation as a practice for good health. It will help you do Pele's work as well. You will become so much more aware of your thoughts and the power of them to create your universe.

The more emotionally sensitive you are as a person, the more that you will feel your thoughts. That is a great thing, because it means when you think a good thought you instantly feel good and you magnetise with your feelings. If you are highly sensitive, you are literally dictating how every fibre of your being feels in every moment by what you are thinking in that moment.

If you are less sensitive, you are still dictating your world with your thoughts. Make sure you are acting in accordance with the thoughts you want to manifest and not contradicting them.

Step Three

Thirdly, choose your thoughts. This is the most powerful thing you will ever do. Your feelings will follow your choice of thoughts. Your words will automatically follow your choice of thoughts. Your actions will follow your choice of thoughts. In the moment that you think great, you will feel great, say something great, do something great and your world will reflect the fact that you are great.

It is time to start feeling your true worth.

The format which I chose for my Memory Inferno is below. You do not have to do it this way if it is not practical to carry this round with you (or a pad). The point of this is that it is an ongoing practice. Any time that you feel a bad feeling or have a negative thought it goes in the Memory Inferno in the left hand column in the past tense. So you have to either write it down in the moment or later that day. You can email yourself or text yourself. If you noticed the bad thought or feeling you are well on your way to feeling great, because you can stop it. You will get better and better at stopping the bad thought train more quickly, and eventually you will catch it before it leaves the station at all. The book is split into areas of your life and each one will be different. In the right hand column write in the present tense to create the thoughts and feelings and things that you want in your life. I have provided some examples in each area but you should write your own.

MEMORY INFERNO *"Right now, I love myself. The work I do in this book makes me love myself more and more all the time."*	
PAST	**NOW AND FOREVER**
	I feel safe
	I feel loved
	I feel happy

3 WHO DO YOU THINK YOU ARE?

The work for this chapter is a general "figuring out" who you have believed you are so far and what or who made you believe that about yourself.

You may know already that you are underconfident in certain situations, or so underconfident you have never done what you want with your life because you are too afraid. But we do not generally go through our day noticing what we are feeling, saying, doing in every moment. You have to start doing this. It is becoming self-aware. If you are reading this you are likely to be in a quiet moment right now, so take the time now to reflect on the last twenty-four hours and think about what you were doing, who you were with, what interactions you had with people or technology (your phone, computer etc). Think about how you felt and what you thought and said.

Write a heading at the top of the page which says: "I believe I am worthy of greatness".

Draw a line down the centre of the page in the Memory Inferno. Negative thoughts and feelings go on the left, positive thoughts and feelings go on the right. A thought which makes you feel nothing or which you had without any real intent, goes on the left. The same goes for the things you say and do, so negative or "nothing" things you said or did go on the left, positive ones on the right.

Label the left hand column "Past", and the right hand column "Now and forever"

Now answer the following questions about that time. If you can remember further, go back further. It is key to write all the things which belong in the left hand column in the past tense. They are what you thought, felt or did in the past.

What things have you said about yourself in that time?

What things have other people said to you or about you?

Do you think you deserve to be happy?

So you may have written on the left "I did not think I deserved to be happy", "I felt shy", "I wanted the ground to open and swallow me up", "I felt overweight", "I felt stupid", "He made me feel like a dumb blond", "I felt inadequate". Just let it all out on the page, in the past tense.

Go deeper

For all the negative things you have written, I want you to now figure out whether you have felt that way at some point before that time. Notice whether when you felt like that, there was a familiar feeling or belief that was triggered. Maybe you were hearing a story or watching something online or television, or a movie, and you felt a bad emotion get triggered. It could be that you felt anger, sadness, frustration, threatened, unsafe, ashamed, or something else that did not feel good.

Can you remember an occasion when you felt that way for the first time?

If you remember one or more previous occasions, write them down in the past tense too. Do not worry if what you write does not make sense right now.

Anything you can remember, write it in your Memory Inferno. However insignificant it seems and whoever or whatever it has to do with, any time you had an opinionated thought, write it down.

Go deeper still

When you have done that, now intensify the process. Think back further over your life. What beliefs have you held about yourself? Do you believe you are healthy and fit, strong and supple, kind and generous, popular and fun, reliable, easy going, wealthy, happy, safe and loved?

Anything positive, write it in the present tense on the right hand side.

If any one of the positive adjectives I used has you cringing at the thought of describing yourself as that, write down any negative adjectives you have used instead to describe yourself, in the past tense on the left hand side.

It is worth spending as long as the words keep coming to mind on this exercise. Write them all down, in the past tense.

This is a broad overview, the tip of the iceberg, of "where you are", in terms of how you feel about yourself and your life. We are going to look at each area of your life in detail like this to figure out where you are in relation to each one.

Then you are going to change how you feel to a more positive frequency. You will literally be changing your life as you do this, from the very moment you change your thoughts, you change your feelings, you change your vibration and you attract great things to you.

In my case, the left hand column for my general overview said "I was suicidal, I tried to take my own life". All the good feelings I may have felt about myself seemed superficial and irrelevant.

Yet I was able to chose to believe in happiness. I am telling you how I got here, because I believe that everyone is capable of being happy and deserves to be happy, that is why we were put on earth, no other reason. If you do not believe that you were meant to be happy, you need to establish why you thought that and let it go.

Notice what area of your life the words you have written in your Memory Inferno relate to. Is it your health? Is it your wealth? Is it your relationships? Is it just an overwhelming feeling of worthlessness?

If it is the latter, you should learn to love yourself because you have a beautiful life waiting for you to start feeling it.

I am going to help you look at each area of your life in more detail in turn.

The aim is to feel love, to really feel love. I do not mean just go out and meet someone to fall in love with, although if you want to then that is likely to follow from Pele's work. What I mean is that being great is about focusing on what you love. Do you want to be great?

If you are not happy, you have not learned what it means to give love. You may think this is patronising, you may be a lot more accomplished than me in life and be more intelligent and/or wealthier than me and/or had several decades of marriage. But if you are not happy now, you are not giving love right now.

BEING GREAT *"I know I am worthy of greatness, I feel it in my bones"*	
PAST	**NOW AND FOREVER**

4 LOVE

When you love yourself, really love yourself, you naturally give love to others and you attract love back to you many times over. Love is hard to describe and is not tangible but you know when you have felt it, it makes you feel wonderful. When you feel it you come alive with it. Realising love is like realising how you are supposed to feel. It is not rational, it is not reasonable, it is just right.

Most of us go through life confused as to what love is. Confusing it with passion and chemistry, deliberately going out to find that as a plaster to stick over our pain. That is not love. Great sex is not love either, it is a temporary high.

The meaning of life is love. I never understood that until recently. Nor did I realise that what I thought was love was not love at all. What I thought was love was actually wrapped up in the projection of different bad feelings I was taught as a child. Each of my parents had taught me as a child that love was passionate and exciting and led to heart break, stress and other disasters. My parents were divorced when I was tiny and I saw my dad, I will call him Kane, after the legendary Pele's father, once or twice a year. I will tell you the story of Kane later on. When I was five, I thought that love was clamouring for attention by achieving things to tell Kane about. It was "absence making the heart grow fonder". It was believing that I was not quite special enough to have someone there for me all the time, or at all. Consequently, I grew up fearing heart break, stress and disaster and seeing love as a big distraction from the practicalities in life. I allowed myself passion and excitement when I did not have a major achievement on the agenda. Those emotions governed every single one of my relationships up until I was in my mid-twenties. Not only that, they governed many other aspects of my life. Did I recognise this? Of course not... I always believed I was right, it was the circumstances that were wrong, or it was the man I chose to blame, for seeing me as an attractive fun person who he had great sex with and great times.

If you are not happy, or you are not feeling much at all, you have to relearn what love is. To do that you have to recognise what it is not. Every thought and action in every moment is governed by what you are feeling, and on the flipside, your feelings reflect the thoughts you are thinking. You have to identify what you are feeling all the time, in all situations and be completely honest with yourself about why you are feeling that way. There is an answer to bad feelings: replace them with something that makes you feel great instead. If you are not doing that all the time and consequently you feel bad, then you need Pele's work.

You can experience love in every moment of every day. That is the meaning of life. We really do attract back to ourselves exactly what we give out. All we have to do is choose to love.

Love is the most powerful feeling that exists. Choose to feel the greatness that is your birth right.

We are going to do the work to figure out where you are with love. The more intelligent you are, the more you may struggle with love. Highly intelligent people often struggle with the concept of love because it is not obviously reasonable and rational. Love does not fit with their logical view of the world, in which everything can be explained intellectually. Love is not visible and it sounds "silly". Therefore people who consider themselves highly intelligent beings often do not like the idea of love. They believe love is for weak or stupid people. In an increasingly competitive world of high achievers, people would sooner believe in the results they can measure by reference to a list of goals which they achieved or cash that they receive, or assets and holidays they can buy with the proceeds of their focus. SMART , as it were.

That is not smart, actually. Often those people settle for rational options instead of what they feel they might love. They may choose an "acceptable" partner, who may or may not be of the sex to which they are attracted, along with "acceptable friends" who they do not love either and they get on with doing mentally stimulating things in life which excite them and therefore distract them from the apparent mundaneness of life. Then one day they break down, because they do not feel anything anymore.

A life without love is darkness personified. That is your very own living inferno.

Intelligent people like to be in charge of their destiny. They make a plan, and focus all their energy on achieving their goals. I know this because I have always been like that. I focus on my goals like a drowning man focuses on getting to the surface of the water to inhale. In other words, nothing gets in my way. Love of course fell in to the "distraction" category. I certainly did not love myself.

What I did not get was that love is the goal. Love is the meaning of life.

If you think you are too clever for love, think again, because the only reason any of us are alive is love. Love really does make the world go around. So it's time to figure out the bad stuff which you keep re-living which is stopping you from feeling love and being love. Leave it in the past, it has gone. You cannot change what has happened, but you can start recognising what you have been doing wrong all this time and stop repeating it, whenever you want to.

You can get out of your own way, right now. Do you want to?

This is what I mean when I say you have to do Pele's work. Pele's work is how you choose love and choose life. You have to acknowledge the things that have made you feel bad up until now and "burn" them in order for you to get out of hell.

You have to learn love, feel love, and give love.

If you feel bad, you are attracting bad things to you all the moments when you are feeling bad.

If you are a high achiever, you may think that you have too much going for you to undo it all. I do not mean to tell you to give anything up that you want in life, I mean to tell you to love yourself.

Ask yourself "Do I feel love when I look at myself in the mirror each morning?". If you do not, then start. If you have done things you feel bad about, maybe so long ago you forgot why you stopped loving yourself, it does not matter. Start loving yourself and evolving everything you do today.

This is a small exercise of giving love to yourself which takes less than a minute:

Look at your hands and say "I love you hands, for just being my hands. I also love all the great things that you do every day".

Look in the mirror and say to your "I love you eyes. I am so happy and grateful that you allow me to see beautiful things."

Rub your ear lobes and say "I love you ears. Thank you for hearing all the wonderful lessons and magical moments which make me wiser and stronger and happy to be alive."

Look at your lips and your mouth and caress your neck and say "I love you voice. Thank you for your mindful expressions of truth and gratitude".

Grin at yourself in the mirror for a minute, grin like you mean it. Notice how it feels, does it feel familiar or alien to you? If you think you look silly it may make you laugh and that is a good thing. Does it make you feel like smiling or laughing? If you cannot feel anything, persevere, you will feel it and then do it naturally. Your grin will make others grin, and you will make friends just going about your routine. You will become persuasive to others and magnetic, just by your heartfelt smile and twinkling eyes.

If you have felt true love, then you know what it is.

If you do not feel much at all on a day to day basis, then you are not loving or living. You do not have to give anything up in order to live, just start loving. The things that are on your new frequency will stay with you, and get even better, the things which are no longer on your frequency will naturally fall away.

Life is love. If you know you are not happy, that is a major acknowledgement and is the first step to happiness. Practice Pele's work.

Everyone can heal, that's how we were made. Just as physical wounds heal, your heart is capable of healing too, if you just let it. What that means is, get out of its way and you will feel what makes you happy. This is "doing Pele's work". It is wiping the slate clean so that you can write magical things on it.

You have to be in the moment, in order to choose happiness in that precise moment. Being truly in the moment means that you are not pre-judging it. You are not projecting your bad feelings on to it as it is happening. If your soul mate wanders past you on the other side of the street, but you are playing "Bad Romance" into your headphones and staring at the pavement while re-living your latest disastrous love affair, your soul mate will pass you by. Is that what you want?

You have to be listening to the joke in order to get it. If you are lost in a bad thought, or you are feeling bad or anxious about something which you think is going to happen, you will not hear the joke. If you do then you will project your bad feelings on to it, then the joke is not funny.

You have to free your mind from the negative shroud in order to experience what is love.

This is true in every area of your life. Health, wealth, relationships, career or work, family, literally everything you experience.

It is critical that you feel love for something in order for it to come to you. Most importantly, love yourself and everything you are.

I was not taught love as a child. There was heart breaking damage done to me as a child but then I continued to behave in ways which just vindicated the damage.

If you can recognise negative behavioural patterns now you can literally change your life. You have to be brutally honest with yourself to do this though. To most of us, bad things that happen and bad people who come in to our lives appear not to be our doing. How can it be your fault that your partner is offensive to you or cheated on you, or lies to you all the time?

Well, you can change it. If you think that you can help a person who treats you badly, you are wrong. You cannot change other people and you are wasting your precious energy trying. You are wasting your love. Give the bad behavior no energy, just leave it behind you.

You can literally stop attracting those people and start attracting people into your life who you love, by turning away from anything that is not love and loving yourself.

I repeatedly attracted men who were wrong for me. This started very early on. At school I had fun attracting boys who played it cool and completely lost interest when they started buying me presents and going all mushy.

The first person I fell in love with was my best friend at school's older brother. I could not have him, because it would have been socially unacceptable, so that made me want him. He was witty and clever. He made fun of me all the time, never showed any affection to me, or indeed anyone (his mother had died when he was a teenager which left him emotionally scarred too). He was the perfect person to project my abandonment issues on to because I would stay in the safe zone, wanting love that I could not have.

I lost my virginity when I was aged fourteen, to a guy who was nineteen and lived 300 miles away from me. I met him on a holiday which my friend's family had taken me on and then when I got home, I persuaded myself that the excitement I felt when I was around him was "love". I went to stay with him. My mum (I will call her Hina after the legendary Pele's mother) rang him up and told him exactly how old I was and that she did not approve. On one view, I was raped, I was drastically under the legal consensual age. On another view, I could blame Hina for letting me go. But the truth is that I put myself in that situation, no one else. I see so clearly now that he was also the perfect projector for my abandonment issues. I slept with a person who I would never get to see and persuaded myself that I loved him. I put myself in a situation that would make me feel the opposite of loved. I regretted losing my virginity even whilst it was happening, I knew he was nothing special and I was not feeling what I thought I felt when we were apart. It was all one big bad projection.

It is easy looking back to when I was fourteen and telling myself I was stupid, but different forms of the same feelings projected themselves over and over again right through into my twenties. I was creating the sensation of love so that it would hurt me, time and again.

I hurt a lot of men who were good to me too through fear of being loved, it was not what I knew about men. I wanted to be used. I had a loving boyfriend in my teens who adored me and respected the fact I was too young to have sex. He put me on a pedestal, he was attractive, kind and generous towards me. My subconscious would not let me fall for him though, so instead I emotionally hurt him to the point of tears, more than once.

I have a string of tales about men I persuaded myself I loved when I was not allowing myself to feel anything close to the power of love. The common feature is that all the men were wrong for me in some way. The string of tales is so long that frankly it would be dull to tell them all. Either the timing was obviously wrong, I could not have them because they had a girlfriend or were married, or they were just ******s, or we were clearly on diverging paths in life. They all ended in tears (mine mainly), via tremendous excitement, a lot of "I love you" and a lot of wild sex. This included married men, obviously the perfect projector for my abandonment issues. That was the feeling I knew, so that is what I stuck to. Kane started a new family instantly at the time he left us. I felt subordinate because he saw them all the time and did not see me at all, so I felt second best. I carried that over into my adult relationships, even having affairs with married men. That was the emotion I knew, love from a man who put his family above me.

I watched Hina do this when I was a child too. Hina had continued her own childhood abandonment issues into her marriage. After Kane left her (or she violently threw him out), she was lost and in pain, having relationships with a number of men at the same time, including a married one.

Through Pele's work I decided to break the chain. I decided I would always love instead. I chose to heal. We can all heal at any time. That is the power of love. We just have to choose it.

Be willing to heal. Respect yourself, love yourself, and the perfect partner for you will appear as if by magic, it is literally that simple. Feel love, and someone on your frequency will come along and reflect it right back to you.

I decided to feel true and real love that empowers me instead of breaks me. I wanted a man who is clever, funny, kind, driven, focused and who I am always learning from and teaching things to. A good person who would be kind to me and respect my career choice. A man I share every day with and everything with. I started to imagine and feel him and have enough faith to clear out the junk, and that is the man who seemed to fall out of the sky and into my arms. I picked him before he appeared in my life. The similarities between our pasts and our personalities were so striking it scared me, as did the intensity of the energy between us. I had never known anyone who understood me the way he did. On the evening that we met, I poured out my life story to him. I came alive in every aspect of my life.

I have continued to heal all the time we have been married and I believe he is my twin flame, we are two parts of the same soul.

Imagine your ideal mate and feel them with all the love that you can muster up. Act like they are already in your life and they will appear.

First, clear out the junk.

Are you ready with your Memory Inferno?

Write a heading at the top of the page which says:

"I am safe and I am loved"

Draw a line down the centre of the page in the Memory Inferno. Negative thoughts and feelings go on the left, positive thoughts and feelings go on the right. A thought which makes you feel nothing or which you had without any real intent, goes on the left. The same goes for the things you say and do, so negative or "nothing" things you said or did go on the left, positive ones on the right.

Label the left hand column "Past", and the right hand column "Now and forever"

Now, write down how you felt in each relationship or sexual encounter you have experienced in the past on the left. There may be a lot, but you have to work through each one. When you have done those, write down how you felt each time you thought you loved someone. How did they make you feel?

You have to completely honest here. If you felt "high" on love, did you feel high all the time or a crashing depression when things felt bad? What was the bad feeling?

Write everything down, in as much detail as you can in the past tense. You can write down the events too, these may be just dates or one night stands, or a series of things in a long relationship.

Now, what you have to do, is figure out the common bad feeling or feelings which are on the left. Let us say you have written "I felt cheap", "I felt used", "I felt humiliated", "I felt angry", "I felt depressed". "I felt lonely".

What are the common feelings in all those experiences? A common bad feeling in love is rejection, or worthlessness. Thinking you love another person but also that they are too good for you and you are so lucky when they call you or give you any attention, but actually they are treating you like you are worthless to them. They seem to have a "hold" over you, some kind of power over you that makes you let them run your life and your feelings.

Write any and all your feelings down. Everything which pops into your head, as soon as it pops into your head. There may be some good feelings you want to take forward with you too, we are coming to those.

Write it all in the left and in the past for now.

If you have never let yourself love anyone, or never opened yourself up to trusting someone else with your feelings, it is time to figure out why that is as well. If you had one sided feelings for someone and never found out how they actually felt or you had some seemingly embarrassing moments, put them in your Memory Inferno.

When the thoughts have stopped popping into your mind and you have stopped writing, read what you wrote.

Go deeper

Have you been honest? If you have not written anything bad down, but someone or something has made you feel bad in the past, you have not been honest. So try again.

When you have written down all your worst feelings and figured out the common ones, what you have to do next is go back to the first occasion when you felt love and there was something bad associated with it.

Maybe there was only one noticeable occasion where you felt something like love for someone and it went wrong and it was not your fault.

If you have never really loved since you felt bad about it, then you are in your own way. You are stopping yourself loving and being loved in return. If you have loved but you think the other person made you feel rejected or worthless, you are wrong.

The truth you have to realise, is no one else can make you feel rejected or worthless, only you have power over your feelings. If you felt rejected, you felt rejected already and someone came along and reinforced what you were feeling about yourself. If you think that it is their fault for treating you in a particular way, it is not their fault.

You have to feel good about you. When you feel good about you no one else can make you feel bad.

We have to love to ourselves in order to attract love. We feel truly happy when we love ourselves, and we attract things we love because love is a magnet.

But what if the feelings that we think are love are fooling us? We were never really taught how to love, or we got heartbroken and never healed.

You have to figure out where the bad feeling first came from, maybe so long ago you have no idea when, and you have to drop the bad emotion into the Memory Inferno.

If someone you love died, that could be something that will choke your heart into fear of ever falling in love again. You have to realise that you are still alive though and you deserve to feel love. The reason you are still alive is to love. That is the only reason for your existence.

Kane died many years ago now. It was the week before Christmas and I flew for 19 hours to visit him in Intensive Care a few days before. He had a stroke there whilst on holiday. He suffered a blood clot when he was too far away from a hospital where they had the facilities to operate to remove it. By the time it was removed a lot of his brain had died.

I arrived in customs and they asked my the purpose of my visit. I couldn't speak, I opened my mouth and a loud wail filled the hall. It felt like everyone was staring at me. I was sobbing uncontrollably.

I arrived at the hospital where the staff were highly competent, and provided us with the hope that he might recover. He couldn't move, talk or breath. I stayed in a hotel near the hospital. I sat by his bed every day, played him classical music, and talked him through physically imagining himself moving again. He occasionally moved one of his hands, and half of his face. It was agony seeing him like that. I still hoped he would recover. It was not the first time he had been in hospital, or the first time he had had a stroke. A few years earlier he had had a triple heart by-pass and had suffered internal bleeding so he had to be re-opened. He suffered a stroke during the procedures and was unconscious for days. Following that he couldn't walk or talk for a while but he recovered to the point where most people would not have known anything had happened, he lost some of his language functions, in particular the foreign languages he spoke, and some of sporting coordination. I realized this time was different. Even if he could recover some of his functions he would not have wanted to live in a wheel chair, unable to talk, sing, play golf, charm the ladies. It would have been no life at all.

Within a week the doctors decided to take him off his breathing support and he died within moments. My younger sister and I were at his bedside.

That night I felt more alone than I had ever been. I was completely devastated.

I experienced extraordinary grief. I got home a few days before Christmas. I cried throughout Christmas. I cried every day for around four months. Then I cried every week for a few months after that. The foundations of my world were shaken. I wasn't just crying, I was shrivelling inside and at times wailing like a baby. I could focus on nothing except the pain I was experiencing. I could not work.

I hung on through the pain, sometimes with the help of one of my favourite songs "Hold on", Wilson Phillips (remember I said not to judge). Three months after Kane died, one of Kane's sisters died of cancer. I felt I could not face another funeral, I was still crying about Kane every day. After three months of crying on the way to work every day, I bumped into an old friend on my way back to work with my lunch. He asked how I was. I started to bawl uncontrollably again.

I love Kane still, he was my best friend and my professional mentor. He had incredibly energy. I still cry occasionally. I feel grief in my dreams. Sometimes I feel his presence in my dreams and they are so colourful and real it is like he is still alive.

It took me years to realise that what I experienced when he died was not simply the grief of Kane dying. It was unprocessed emotions from when he left when I was four years old. Of course I hadn't processed those emotions, I was four.

With that realisation, came a flood of realisations about other emotions and patterns. Emotions and behaviours I had been living my entire life. They were the life I had created for myself.

I put those feelings into my Memory Inferno. I gave them to Pele and she burnt them alive for me. The hardest thing was actually recognising what I had been doing my whole life. But when you finally see the pattern, it is so obvious.

If you feel that you are in a bad relationship, remember that there is no point in judging other people for their behaviour in a relationship with you, just let it go and recognise that you are different now. You choose to feel good. You therefore attract other people who are on your feel good frequency.

You may think you cannot trust another person again because someone or many people treated you so badly. You can trust yourself now though. Put mistrust into the Memory Inferno. As soon as you love you and feel good, you will recognise people who are not in a good place and you will just give them no energy. You will not be vulnerable to being treated badly anymore. They will not get your number in the first place and have no opportunity to bring your good feelings down.

Once you have let your bad feelings from the past go, you will already feel better. Your Memory Inferno should be filled with things which you associated love with but which made you feel bad. Now you can set your heart alight with love and allow yourself to feel passion, not plasters.

I had on the left "I felt lonely", "I felt hurt", "I felt neglected", "I felt heartbroken", "I felt rejected", "I felt I could not trust anyone with my heart", "I felt worthless".

On the right it says "I feel love", "I feel loved", "I love myself", "I love other people", "I feel happy", "I feel accepted", "I deserve love". As you write the positive affirmations on the right hand side, feel them and imagine what impact they are having on your life as you write them. As you feel and imagine that, write more positive things down and get more specific about what makes you feel great.

LOVE *"I am safe and I am loved"*	
PAST	**NOW AND FOREVER**

5 WEALTH

Money does not make you happy. But we need it to do what we want most of the time. You should know that the key to being rich is feeling rich. The key to always having enough money, is feeling and knowing that you always have enough money to do whatever you want all of the time. If you feel a lack of money in your life, or you feel that your work is not "valued" in monetary terms, guess what you are doing? You are asking the universe to confirm your beliefs. You should know this already, but if you do know this or you have read it and you still feel bad about money then you need Pele.

I absolutely do not mean you have not gone out and earned money or tried to get a job. I mean you have not figured out why you feel bad about money and burnt it alive.

I was poor, really poor. To the point where I felt embarrassed about it all of the time at school. I was the poor kid in a wealthy neighbourhood. I had no lunch money when other kids were feasting at lunch time, I could not afford to go on the school trips because they were aimed at parents with money. I could not afford the school uniform. I was highly energetic and talented at sport but could not afford most of the kit or training. To me that was hell on earth.

I am what I would describe as wealthy now. I feel great about money and I feel happy and secure. Money does not make you happy of itself, we can all see that. I already owned a beautiful home with no mortgage on it and had a flash car when I tried to end my time on this earth. I am not unique, there are many examples of rich people who succeed in killing themselves. You can be both rich and happy though. Money certainly does not make you miserable. A myth Hina tried to teach me was that "money is the root of all evil", it was virtually her favourite phrase. I think this may have come from the fact that her own father had wealthy parents and he made nothing of himself. He was absent from her childhood in the same way Kane was from mine, also having had another family.

Money may *appear to be* a source of your unhappiness or stress in your life, and if it is, you can change that belief. As long as you get stressed about it, you send out that vibration to the universe and bring in stresses and worries about it. As long as you resent or hate rich people, you are rejecting money, literally repelling it with your feelings.

When you feel good about money, you will attract money and you will feel better and better about money, thereby attracting more of it. This too is an area where you first have to do Pele's work. Figure out how it is you do not feel good about money, what thoughts and feelings you are experiencing which are in your way?

When I was about twelve, living with Hina and my older sister, I remember Hina telling us that she had gone bankrupt. I remember how desperate she was leading up to that point and how resigned she was to that fate. She was sending out damsel in distress vibes to the universe and they were reflecting right back at her. The bank forced a sale on the house, when the nineties recession had already hit so the house had negative equity.

This seemed to have an extraordinarily bad emotional effect on me. It also put a huge strain on an already fraught relationship with Hina. I blamed Hina. I was truly angry for the first time in my life and I would not let go of it for over ten years.

I also felt humiliated and embarrassed, even more so than ever before. We had nowhere to live. Hina could not actually afford to rent anywhere. She took a six month lease on a house nearby, but she could not pay the rent during that period. We moved on to another place where she also could not pay the rent, and overstayed there for around two years.

I felt so "out of control" that I was anorexic and bulimic for a time. My grades dropped at school, I was consumed by a feeling of complete insecurity and helplessness.

There was a period in my teens I had no toothpaste, shampoo, soap, food, hot water, heating, or electricity. I felt dirty, embarrassed and worthless.

At that point I was sharing a bed with Hina, as it was a two-bedroom house. Hina was claiming benefits and legal aid, in a case against Kane which was consuming her with rage. She refused to go to work at that point because of the benefits she would lose. I felt like part of unit that was a complete drain on society and I could not wait to get out.

I feel extremely blessed that the state paid for people to go to university at that time. As soon as I graduated I bought my own flat. Finally I had a salary and my own home and I felt a huge sense of relief that I could look after myself. I kept many of these habits and emotions for years afterwards though. Like both of my parents, I got credit cards and spent far too much on them.

In my twenties I developed a habit of buying way more household goods than I actually needed. Shampoo, conditioner, soap, shower gel, cleaning products, sanitary products, food.

My anorexia passed as I became more accomplished and felt safer and more secure, but in its place I developed other anxiety illnesses: serious gut problems and obsessive compulsive disorder. I know now that these illnesses were all in my thoughts and emotions. They were just the stored trauma of feeling desperately out of control.

I know from my experience that it is possible to heal and feel amazing instead.

Write a heading at the top of this Memory Inferno which says:

"I am wealthy, prosperous, safe and secure. I always have enough money to do whatever I want"

Write your past emotions in the past column, in the past tense. Write some positive affirmations like the ones below on the right hand side. Really feel them and believe them as you write them, they should fill you with joy.

"I am wealthy, prosperous, safe and secure. I always have enough money to do whatever I want"	
PAST	**NOW AND FOREVER**
	I feel excited about money
	I feel provided for
	I feel wealthy
	When I receive bills, I feel grateful for what I received in return and I always just pay them
	I feel my unique talent is valued by society
	I always find a win-win and get paid fairly for what I give
	I am overflowing with valuable ideas which I act on
	I have the confidence to do what I love and make others love it too
	I give to others from a feeling of my own abundance

6 HEALTH

The focus for your learning is loving you. The areas of your life which appear to you to need fixing are not broken like a smashed glass, they need love and they will heal.

I can say from my own experiences that all of the illnesses I have had in my life were a reflection of my poor mental and emotional health at the time. I had a complete lack of love for me. I have already mentioned the anxiety disorders I experienced for almost two decades, culminating in my failed suicide attempt. There were many many, many illnesses I had as a child at school that no one else in the school ever got. I was frequently in the doctors with a number of doctors surrounding me. Some of these were simply genetic: I have a "spare rib" which pokes out of my neck, and a "text book" cataract in my left eye which was found when I was about 4 years old. I had the usual illnesses too, flu, chicken pox, measles, whooping cough. But I was the only child I have ever known to have pityriasis rosea, and both chicken pox and shingles (in fact I do not know another child who has had shingles), and two different types of glandular fever. The point is that I felt emotionally traumatized, therefore I became ill.

I had so many traumatic experiences on holiday that I stopped having holidays as an adult for a time as I associated them with stress and trauma. I used to cry as the plane left the runway. I was stung in the sea by a Portuguese man o war (again, the only child I know, there were hundreds of other people swimming in the same place), I almost drowned in a swimming pool (a stranger thought I was annoying and forced my head under water until I choked and I cried hysterically for the rest of the day), I dropped a breeze block on my foot causing my toenail to fall off, I got stuck up a mountain in a storm on a rock face with no equipment and hung there for an hour whilst the mountain rescue came to get me down (again, I was screaming hysterically for an hour). Now you could put all these traumas down to coincidence if you wanted to. But I firmly believe that I attracted these with my pre-existing state of trauma. I was already in an emotionally traumatized place, which is like asking the universe to send trauma your way. If you are stressed, you attract things which appear stressful. If you focus on problems, you get more of them.

I have literally changed the way that my body feels and is by re-training my conscious and subconscious.

The key is first feeling healthy. You are what you feel you are. The start of feeling it is imagining it. If you have never been healthy you do not know what it feels like to be healthy, you have to start by imagining it until you feel it. Then live it.

The most effective way to allow yourself to imagine and feel things is in a state of deep relaxation which can be achieved through meditation. When you meditate frequently and effectively, you will become far more relaxed all of the time, even when you are not meditating. When you are relaxed, it is easy to make great and transformative things happen.

I can give you a simple tangible example of a common problem: a wart. I had a wart on my finger for years. I tried everything to get rid of it, every so called miracle wart treatment on the market. It would not shift. The more I tried, the more frustrated I got. The more frustrated I got, the more I tried treating it. I was stuck in this rut of focusing on the wart and how ghastly it was and that it would not go.

Then I tried not treating it, and instead, every morning and evening, without applying any treatment, I looked at my finger and I said "thank you God for my healthy, flawless, beautiful hands" over and over again. My finger literally just healed on its own. No joke. The key was focusing on what I wanted, a healthy finger, instead of the very thing I did not want.

I have a very similar story about a fungal toe nail which I treated unsuccessfully for years with every available treatment on the market. I focused on a healthy beautiful toe nail and now I have it.

Focus on a healthy, energetic, beautiful, glowing you and really feel and believe it, and that is exactly what will look back at you in the mirror.

I focus on health now. I have a healthy diet and exercise routine, I practice yoga and meditation, I sleep properly and I feel calm under enormous pressure at work.

In order to do this it is important to make it a practice. The more you are aware of what you are thinking and feeling the more you can change. The best way to set your mind up for the day is a morning meditation. There are hundreds of different meditations in different media out there, apps, podcasts, audio programs, books. If you start the day thinking how wonderful today is going to be, the universe gives you a wonderful day.

If you are new to meditation you could start by reading this to yourself every morning:

Good morning.
Thank you universe for blessing me with this beautiful day,
filled with wonderful experiences that make me feel fantastic and grateful to be alive.
Thank you for my perfect health and high energy levels.
Thank you for my beautiful unique body.
Thank you for the food I eat which is perfectly assimilated in my body and makes me feel fantastic.

Write your own gratitude meditation which gives thanks for the things you want. If you want to be a supermodel, give thanks for your supermodel looks. If you want to be super fit, give thanks for the fact you are super fit. As you are giving thanks, really feel what you are saying thank you for.

Do you feel great? Can you remember the last time you felt great? You should know what it means for you to feel great, and you should know why you felt great. If you have never felt great, start learning about things that make other people feel great.

The reason for many pains in the body are because we focus on them, they are a check for the fact that we are not being mindful of what we want. We are instead focusing on something negative, or not letting go of something in the past. The philosophy behand yoga and pilates, is to set the pain free and focus on positive movement and action instead. For example, a pain may be caused by the unique way in which your body moves. With pilates you can train the muscles to move in a different way which is pain free. It literally shifts the body's focus from the pain to a positive way of moving. If we do nothing and focus on the pain instead, it just gets worse. Focusing on pain is asking for more pain.

Most people are walking around with some kind of pain. It is often stored tension and stress that we have not let out. We store tension in our bodies. Tension leads to pain. Pain is often a metaphor or an alarm bell which is telling you something emotionally, but we do not really listen to what our bodies are telling us, we go to the doctor for a quick fix so that we can get on with not feeling anything. Yoga is fantastic for setting free tension stored in the body, clearing the mind and making space for greatness.

Before you feel a really bad pain, you will have many warning symptoms from your body, and you probably do not feel those warning signs, or you do feel them and you choose to ignore them.

Have you ever watched a person being shouted at and observed what happens to their body? In particular a child. A child being shouted at screws up their face, tenses up their arms and shoulders and may start crying to let out the pain caused by the person shouting at them. As adults we do not tend to react so obviously to emotional stressors, but there is nevertheless physical tension caused by our daily experiences and it gets stored in our bodies. We grind our teeth in our sleep, or we get very stiff and inflexible in certain parts of our bodies (for example the hips, neck and shoulders). There is a correlation between how we physically feel and the mental and emotional experiences we have. If we do not let out this out it simply stays in the body, causing imbalance, pain and illness.

Have you ever watched a person who hates public speaking giving a speech to a hundred people? They sweat, they shake, their voice becomes shakey and sounds different. There are physical effects from our thoughts and emotions. Our thoughts and emotions physically present themselves in the world, both in our bodies and in everything we experience.

If you have never tried yoga, or never clicked with yoga, it is a magical way to reconnect with yourself and to learn to love your body. You may not believe you have a soul but it does not really matter, you will start to feel anyway. My husband declares that he does not believe humans have souls. I feel his warm and generous love all the time. He picked me up from work today and told me he had bought me a present. It is not a special occasion, he just did. As I smiled and kissed him I suddenly noticed two men in business suits standing outside Goldman Sachs watching us and I could see in their faces that they saw the love too. We are all put on this earth to love, no other reason, we are made up of love. By learning to love yourself you are restoring yourself to the perfect being that you are intended to be.

Yoga will light up the real you. You just have to find a style that works for you.

Yoga changed me and my attitude and my life in ways which I would have to write another book about to explain. This book is not about yoga and does not seek to make you love yoga in the way that millions of people round the world today do, but before I move off the topic altogether, I will just say the following: 1) You do not have to "believe" in anything to do yoga and to feel the benefits straight away. 2) Yoga can physically heal a broken heart. In the language of chakras it can "open a heart chakra" that has been closed and has felt nothing for years, whether you believe you have a heart chakra or not. It reaches through your body and mind to your soul. Finally, 3) Nowadays you do not have to physically go to a class, you can receive classes via an app on your phone or laptop.

"I am perfectly healthy"	
PAST	**NOW AND FOREVER**
	I always feel fantastic

	I love my body
	I feel youthful, fit and flexible
	I am always calm
	I only focus on what is good for me

7 CAREER

You do not have to give up your life to make it happy, just do what you love. If you do not know where to start… start loving you. You will figure out from there what you love. That might be the career you have already, using the same skills that (if you are like me) you worked thousands of hours gaining. You may be awesome at your job, but currently feel nothing for it. There may be aspects of it which you don't love. You may think you hate the people you work with, or that they hate you. You may think that there is no point in your work at all but you do not know what else you would do. Hating other people is just a feeling of hatred inside you somewhere. That is all it is. If you can figure out what that feeling really is about and let it go, there will be no hatred in your world. This of itself will make you feel infinitely better about whatever you do. That is where to start.

Wherever you are, do not judge yourself for it. Start loving you instead. Start loving everything you do. Before you do anything, feel love.

I have spent decades working hundred-hour weeks in the same field of work, building up respect, becoming excellent at what I do, doing an excellent job every time and being a hundred per cent reliable. I know that I help people by providing valuable services to them. I am instructed by professional in my field to do the really difficult stuff which they either hate doing, or cannot do. I solve hugely stressful problems for people and seemingly play a big role in changing their lives. As a result of unwavering focus, drive and determination, I have built up a superb reputation. I am not going to give this up anytime soon, but you can imagine it is pretty heavy going. I thought this was acceptable because I thought "No one climbs Everest smiling, right". I have built my practice from the ground up, giving every client I represent the best I can do.

I was absolutely not *loving it* though. Quite the opposite. I gave everything to my work, to the point there was no energy left for "me". I made absolutely no time for me. I ground myself down to the point of "me" being unrecognizable. Worse still, there were negative emotions from my childhood and my experiences in the workplace early on in my career which were driving me. Driving me never to feel vulnerable, never to feel bullied, never to be made to feel like a useless sex object. But the more I resisted, the more the feelings I was running from persisted.

I had a boss once who I felt was a chauvinist pig and treated me like a beautiful object there to serve him. I did not realise that actually it was me who felt like that. If I had not felt like that then he could not have made me feel like I was being used. I would not have taken his attitude towards women personally. I don't think his behavior was acceptable, on the contrary, but I need not have got so upset about it: Everyone else saw it anyway and he was fired from the firm after I left.

I strove hard to achieve one thing after another. I did not understand that no amount of achievement would make me feel better unless I started from the right feeling. The thousands of hours I have spent gaining skills and knowledge serve me well now, but they are not what made me great at what I do. We can only serve other people to the best of our ability when we put ourselves first. Only when we feel great can we truly be great.

If any of this sounds familiar to you, you need Pele.

I found Pele. I figured out what the bad things driving me to succeed were, and I dropped them. I burnt them, instead of them burning me out.

That does not mean achieving less, or not setting goals anymore, on the contrary. Once you drop the bags full of manure in the right place, roses grow. You live in the moment, and joy drives your focus. It is like seeing something extraordinarily beautiful that you cannot take your eyes off, like a blanket of stars on a warm summer night. That is very different to what I was doing, which was blocking out the world and all its beauty in order to achieve things and feeling utterly exhausted all of the time.

Imagine the bad feelings you felt in the past as horse manure. They came from somewhere and they are a part of life but they need to be recycled. You need to drop the manure on the flower bed, and watch the roses grow. Let the bad stuff go and allow the good stuff to happen. Focus on what you love about your work and give no energy to the rest of it.

If you work for clients and you only have limited time and resource, drop the ones who do not float your boat, and give more to the ones who do. I work for clients who I admire and respect, some who I am in awe of. They make me part of things projects which I am really proud to be a part of.

Be on the frequency of love. Take your responsibilities lightly. Start to love *how good you are* at your job. Respect who you are and what you are capable of. Be confident in every situation. Recognise and love the skills you have, and use them for what you love.

If you have felt thus far like your career or work, or life, has been a struggle, look at what you love and take that forward. Leave the rest behind. Stop struggling, stop feeling bad, stop hating it. If you feel like you have not learned anything worth knowing so far in life, that is not true either, because you now know what you do not love. You have seen the cave. The cave had an entrance and it has an exit too. Use the exit.

If you feel like people do not give you the respect you have earned: start respecting yourself and your work more. Demand that respect, know that you deserve it. You have to start asserting yourself from a feeling of self-worth. If you do not do that, you will watch other people with less talent but more confidence getting ahead of you.

In my twenties I worked for two large corporations. Each of them was entirely male dominated, not a single woman in a management role, and in one of them (a large American bank) many of the departments did not have a single woman. Looking around me I felt that there were a lot of men who had been doing not a lot for several decades and being paid more than the rest of the market for the same role. There were male cliques and there was bullying and degrading treatment of the few women there. This of course resonated with my childhood fears and emotions in a negative way. The cultural rule of thumb in the said large American bank appeared to be "He who shouted loudest won the day", regardless of whether he was shouting anything worth hearing. Added to that, I was attractive and so I was "objectified" by the men in meetings and made to feel like a distraction rather than an asset.

I now know that the truth is I did not need to feel like that, no one can make you feel anything. That behavior is the focus of the person dishing it out. It does not need to be your focus. Focus on your own ability and talent, and your focus will shift everyone else's focus to your ability and the work that you are doing. You do not need to try to stamp out demeaning behavior, just give it no energy by focusing with all your might on what is great about you.

I realise this may be easier said than done in extreme situations. A lot of our reactions to situations appear to be hormonal and feel like we have no control over them. They seem to trigger our "fight or flight" mode. I once walked into a meeting with my boss and he was finishing a meeting with another person, a friend of his (I will call him "Zed", a villain from one of my favourite films) who had worked at the bank for fifteen years. I was new there. I was wearing a black trouser suit. Zed stopped what he was saying, looked me up and down and said "You are looking very sexy today".

I do not know exactly what happened to me in that moment I just know this: Zed made me see red. The words which came out of my enraged but still face were simply "get out, now".

There was a silence which felt like it lasted an hour and I stared hard at Zed. Then Zed looked at my boss. My heart was beating fast as I wondered whether my boss was Maynard, Zed's underrated brother and partner in crime. My boss said calmly to Zed "I think you had better go". I proceeded with my meeting in a highly focused and professional manner, my heart still beating fast. Then I returned to my desk. The moment I sat down and reflected on Zed's comment I was filled with rage, I reported the incident and my opinions on Zed's professional capability to the head of Europe the Middle East and Asia, also a man. Who knew what he would do. Had I earned enough respect from the work I had done not to be labelled a trouble maker? This could have a murderous effect on my still budding career and reputation in the bank.

As it happened, my boss was apparently not Maynard. There were some heated meetings in the glass rooms at the edge of the department to which I was not invited, and shortly thereafter, Zed left the building and never returned.

As time went on at the bank, I discovered that others had had professional and personal problems with Zed. They thanked me personally for apparently ending Zed's long career at the bank and I made friends.

I was relatively junior and of course there is a fear that if you speak out no one will want to listen to you, and in an environment where there are no senior women that the men will stick together as they have always done. But where there is change there is always fear.

You have to be the change. Be the light that guides everyone else through into a better world. To do this you have to love and respect you and everything that you do.

I know that the years I have slaved away have made me very knowledgeable and skilled at what I do. I just needed to realise that it was time to feel great and work for people and causes I believe are great. No one can love acquiring knowledge and skills for the sake of it. For me that meant in practical terms doing the same specialist work but entirely differently and with new skills. I am still learning new skills and building knowledge every day. The difference is I feel great, and it is reflected back at me through happy and grateful clients.

Maybe you are in that boat, or maybe you are somewhere else learning things you never want to experience ever again. You are where you are and it is time to start loving each day.

Nothing is wasted if you choose love right now. If you think about it, people who have been in the same career for fourty years would not be successful if they were just relying on knowledge they learned when they first began, we have to grow and change and learn every day otherwise the world moves past us. The most successful people accelerate their rate of learning all the time. It's learning quickly that makes us continually successful. Grow with your heart leading the way.

Pele's work for this chapter is to notice what negative feelings you have about colleagues, clients, activities, any apparently external triggers in your work. Maybe you are not at work or you are self-employed and you would like different clients. What are the negative feelings? Write them all in the past tense in the left hand column.

I started this chapter telling you I used to work myself into the ground. The emotions that went with this were a real rollercoaster. I used to have shouting voices in my head all day making me focus on complex matters to meet drafting deadlines, I used to feel that I had to control everything at a micro level and would spend unnecessary time on unimportant issues that would go unnoticed. In other words I had obsessive tendencies that were not productive. The fact that your work feels out of control and you feel the need to obsess over it is essentially a reflection of the fact you feel out of control and anxious and have an obsessive need to control things.

You have to shift your energy to a higher more positive frequency and only focus on what actually needs doing for a successful outcome. Focus on winning. Focus on feeling great and great work will flow out. Basically, do not start anything unless you feel focused on success.

You may get obvious signs in the morning that you are rushing and you are a bit out of sorts. You spilled your breakfast, forgot something, tripped up. If you feel like that, literally stop and take a moment, breath and refocus your energy. If you are shattered, do not judge it and do not push yourself to do the impossible that day because you are likely to just create more work for yourself and other people. Feel great, then start afresh.

The perfect way to feel great in the morning is with a gratitude meditation to give thanks for all the wonderful things that you want to experience that day as though they have already happened. You literally create your day this way.

This is just a different example to the one starting on page 27.

Morning mediation:
Thank you for my perfect health and high energy levels today.
Thank you for inspiring me to have great ideas.
Thank you for putting me in exactly the right places at exactly the right moments with exactly the right people today to make my ideas manifest.

Thank you for making me aware and alert to opportunities so that I seize them when I sense the time is precisely right.

Thank you for the miracles.

Below is a sample of Pele's work for this chapter, for you to complete with the bad feelings you have felt in the past tense on the left, and your intentions for the future in the right hand column in the present tense.

"I am successful in everything I do"	
PAST	**NOW AND FOREVER**
	I feel totally confident in every situation
	I am always in the right place at the right time
	I always have great inspiration and ideas
	I always follow my instincts and see the right ideas through
	I know I always do a great job
	I know my abilities and actions are valued
	I have great relationships with all of my colleagues
	I do my work effortlessly and with joy

8 RELATIONSHIPS

There are two lessons for this chapter.

One, the world is you, reflected back at you.

Two, you cannot change other people. In other words, you have to change you. Everything else will fall in to place because everything in your life is how you feel, reflected back at you.

Everyone in your life is a projector for how you feel. If you feel great, your relationships will feel great too. You will attract positive constructive people in everything you do. Socially, in your career, your family relationships, everything.

Have your Memory Inferno to hand, and write down all the negative things you feel about all the people you interact with. Do you feel victimized or overly criticized? Do you get fixated on certain personality traits (these are the things you fear about yourself)? Do you feel disappointed or let down by other people? If you do not feel anything for other people, ask yourself whether you have stopped feeling altogether? Look around at your relationships and the people you interact with daily. Do they feel special to you? Do you take people for granted? Do you ever try and make others feel bad to try to make yourself feel better? Are you even aware of how you make other people feel? Do you feel afraid to get close to other people or let them know how you feel?

Go through the same exercise here as you went through for Love. Write down every negative feeling. Include in this feelings of judgement of other people, you do not need these either.

Do you feel insecure or vulnerable? Do you feel bullied in everyday situations? Bullied by large corporates? Powerless? Do you feel like there is someone in the workplace who has a power over you? Include your boss in this because actually they do <u>not</u> have power over you, only you do. You should not feel like your boss has any kind of power over you. If you do feel that way, it is a projection of an emotion you are feeling quite apart from how your boss makes you feel.

When you are done writing and the thoughts have stopped, read them back again.

Now: Go deeper.

Can you remember times in your earlier life when you felt that way?

I was bullied as a child, in a persistent manner by someone I could not escape from. Someone Hina protected each time she did something awful, including to me. She was a lot bigger and taller than me, vicious and nasty. I felt completely powerless at that time. The times in my adult I felt powerless, I had no need to, they were a projection of early stored trauma.

There were so many other bad feelings from circumstances throughout my childhood which were completely outside my control that each of them compounded the others. So I spent my childhood hoping that one day I would be as far away from it as possible.

Most of the time I used these negative feelings to gain security and status, to make me feel secure and in control. Running away from these bad feelings drove me to a certain point in my career, but as I have already said, they did not get me to my power and they almost saw me off the earth.

When I gave these negative feelings to Pele, she made them sound trivial (that's a metaphor for writing them in the memory Inferno). I wonder now, why did I let them govern me for a moment, let alone for decades?

Letting the past go and loving you will automatically change all of your daily interactions with other people and everything that you do.

You may notice more how some of the people around you treat you as well. If you have been in a bad place it is likely that you have surrounded yourself with people who do not love and respect you. You cannot expect other people to change with you though, so if you notice people are treating you badly, just shift your focus to other people.

Hurt people hurt people. It may sound cliched, but it is true.

People who lash out, or manipulate and abuse others are in a bad place themselves. Sometimes you have to accept that you cannot help other people and if a relationship is draining you, you have to walk away from it, even though it hurts you to do that. The fact that you cannot change people means that you cannot help them either.

I had a close friend at school who had always struggled with anorexia and depression. I did too when I was at school. She did not escape it and turned to drugs when she left school before ending her own life in her prime.

One day she left an incoherent drunken message on my mobile in the middle of the day which was abusive towards me. I was upset and distressed by it and made a decision that day not to return her calls. She went into rehab and she came out but relapsed and killed herself. This is tragic, but I could not have saved her.

She should have had a great life. She was highly intelligent, beautiful, wealthy and loved. If someone does not want to feel great even when they are great, you cannot make them feel great. You cannot change another person's feelings about themselves. Most of all, you must not feel guilty for the way that another person feels. You are not responsible for how they feel, they are.

It is really important that you deal with your childhood emotions in your Memory Inferno. Things which sound trivial were not trivial to your childhood emotions if you remember them. Most people know on the whole whether their childhood was happy or unhappy. If I try to summarise my childhood feelings it is easy to do and probably sounds totally cliched.

I felt abandoned by my parents and I felt hated, assaulted and bullied by my older sister. I felt poor. I felt I could not rely on anyone but myself. I felt I could not escape my situation because I was only a child therefore I felt trapped and helpless. I could not earn money (I got a paper round when I was ten, having lied to the shop owner about my age, but he was so nice I confessed to him after the first day and gave him back the money). I could not get new parents who cared about me. I felt I could not get my family to love me. So I felt stuck and worthless.

I grew up in the same house as a sister who was almost three years older than me. I only remember the bad things she did to me. It is possible there were nice things and I don't recall them. The bad things are horrible. Hateful, spiteful, manipulative, jealous, lying and violent. I do not speak to her anymore. That is a permissible choice about which I feel good and empowered. There are relatives who have tried to make me feel guilty about this choice because they feel sorry for her. I do not feel guilty because I know from many years of trying that I cannot help her. Only she can help her.

You must always choose love. If you give love in a relationship and it is lost, or something bad is thrown back at you, that is not your fault and you can choose to leave. You cannot change another person, but you can walk away from the relationship and give them no energy. It is important that if you help people, you do not feel bad trying to do that. All you can do is give love. If other people make you feel bad when you are giving them love, put your energy elsewhere.

In the legend of Pele, Pele is a fire goddess who travelled to Hawaii on a canoe made by her older brother, Ka-moho-alii ("Ka"), the dragon or king of the sharks. He was a favorite of the fire-goddess Pele. Na-maka-o-ka-hai, "Namaka", a sea-goddess, as a result of family trouble, became Pele's most bitter enemy, fighting her with floods of water, according to the legends.

Pele's household represented the two eternal enemies, fire and water. Pele also had a younger sister who travelled with her in the canoe, Hi-iaka (she was called Hi-iaka I-ka poli o Pele, meaning Hi-iaka in the bosom of Pele).

I will call my older sister Namaka. I do have a younger sister and brother too, they do not speak to Namaka either. Namaka is like a highly destructive sea storm and when you have felt the force of her you want to live in peace and hope the storm never happens again.

Pele's father Kane was one of the four great gods of Polynesia, Ku, Kane, Lono, and Kanaloa. Kane might be interpreted as "Kane, the divine companion or friend." A better rendering is "Kane, the divine fire-maker." I have been calling my own dad Kane in this book. He is my hero and fire starter. I have talked about his absence from my childhood and his death but not his love. I began to have a relationship with him when I was in my late teens, and by the time he died almost twenty years after that, I knew that he loved me with all his heart. Kane had a huge heart. He was a sensitive romantasist. He read and wrote poetry and loved gardening, flower arranging, opera and ballet. He was highly cultured, well travelled and intelligent. He was sociable and charming and generous to a fault. He was also very spiritual. I will share with you a poem that he wrote for me.

A Midnight Prayer ©

O' fair limbed form whose grace and beauty wed
This night of velvet blue and twinkling gems
To thy sweet sleep on linen painted with
A scene and dream of peace so rare – wake not!

Still in thy sleep hold the childlike prayer of
This frail heart – that whenst this silver dream which
Nature brought through moon so bright and face so
Fair, harsh daylight breaks – the world of man
Will not transform our hope into the coldest
Dust of day – power, vain greed, the basest brass
And day which in his brutal world man doth
Engage – these have no place where moon and
Stars and your fair form by nature cradled
In a sleep of peace so fill a heart with
Steely hope and thenst our dream with gentle care.

Sleep on sweet night and maid so fair and may
You never see a world of lesser beauty nor

Of truth, for when thou wak'st these words shall form
A shield which thou can'st wear as heart and emblem
Of your father's love; quietly but with strength
And laughter, clearly, on the sleeve of waking life!

I love this poem. In my adult life, Kane was my career mentor and best friend. I totally adored him, I still do even though he has passed. I feel his presence with me always.

Namaka would not let Kane love her. I do not think she knows love. She acted like she hated Kane. Namaka was apparently dissatisfied from birth. Hina says that when Namaka was a baby, Namaka was always crying. Apparently once she cried so long and hard that Hina had to walk round the block because the noise was so disturbing.

My earliest memory of Namaka's effect on me, is of an incident when I was around three years old. Hina had taken me to the local doctor, not because I was in any pain but with whom she had decided that my left leg would not grow straight unless it was trained by large heavy poles of metal strapped to the whole lower half of my body. I remember emerging out of the front door to our house, onto the garden, wearing the metal contraption. Kane was gardening, a great hobby of his, and Namaka was standing there.

Within an instant, there was a long gangly arm pointing at me and a laughing screech which could have deafened the neighbours. I burst into hysterical tears and retreated rapidly into the house to remove the said metal contraption. I never wore it again. I was afraid of Namaka because she was violent, angry and bigger than me. I had good reason to be afraid because she was always doing things to hurt me or my feelings with very bad intent. These incidents started out fairly mildly and got worse as we got older.

When I was about four, Kane was in hospital for a time. We went to visit him and stayed in a hotel. I had a security blanket, it was pink, soft and woven and I carried it everywhere, nestling my face into it. When we left the hotel I noticed immediately that it wasn't in the car. I checked the seats, and the boot, and started crying that it wasn't in the car. Hina and Namaka unpersuasively but aggressively assured me that it was in the car boot. I knew they were both lying. I never saw my blanket again. Putting this in my Memory Inferno I recognised that although this sounds utterly trivial, I have been carrying feelings of insecurity that are completely unnecessary, feelings like someone is going to come along and steal what comforts me. That was the first incident I can remember of that in my childhood.

Kane came out of hospital.

Kane was seriously fun and I worshipped him. I was very active and so was he. He had put a large tyre hanging from a tall old oak tree in the garden on a very long rope, and erected swings. He used to take me up the apple tree in the garden to collect apples which Hina used to bake with. He took me for walks in the woods at the end of the road. He put me on his shoulders and ran with me. He took me swimming. Everything he did with me was exciting and fun. He was the life force in the household. He was my best friend.

What followed was another affair by Kane. I remember an incident where Hina was screaming at Kane. It was possibly boxing day. I thought it was my birthday because Hina had told me that my birthday was "after Christmas". I could not get a more accurate response from her. This sounds quite funny to me now but I was very inquisitive as a child and I Hina could not answer most of my questions so my head was filled with a lot of responses I did not understand, because they made no sense. When I was growing up Google was not on tap and there were no books in our house. I felt frustrated a lot of the time.

Back to the chronology. Hina was violently screaming at Kane in the kitchen. I knew something was very very wrong. Hina's screaming was irretrievably out of control. I loved Kane so much I could not bear the thought of him going away. I ran into the kitchen crying to try to stop the fighting but it didn't distract them at all. Kane wiped avocado off his suit which Hina had thrown at him. He was calm, but horrified and disgusted.

Kane left.

In that moment, I felt abandoned, unloved, unacknowledged. I blamed Hina for screaming and being violent towards Kane. Hina scared me as well but Hina was overwhelmingly sad. Hina plainly felt abandoned and unloved.

Everything was upsetting to me at that time. I attended nursery reluctantly, and felt like I was "left out" of everything. I was frequently told to play on my own as there was only room for three people in the sand pit. I just felt devastated, sitting on my own, sulking.

I started primary school and was shy and lacking confidence. Even though I was talented at everything. I was the fastest runner in the school and the best at maths. So lacking in confidence was I that when I got to the finish line of the egg and spoon race and it was so quiet all around me, I thought I was doing the race wrong. I stopped and turned around to see where the other kids were and of course dropped my egg. Meanwhile two kids came past me and I realised I had just been the fastest by a stretch. I heard my grandma screaming at me about how stupid I was from the side line. I got it together and came third.

Activities at school were a distraction from how sad I felt. I didn't experience the joy of being a child. Given how easy I found everything at school, this is a great shame. I wished I went to a school where it was all work and sport, and no down time. I desperately wanted to go to boarding school but neither of my parents could afford it.

When Kane left, the arrangement was that we would see him for one weekend every month. Namaka refused to go. My step mother evidently could not stand the sight of me in the house and would act as though I was not there, refusing to respond to me and completely ignoring me in an angry fashion.

One day Kane did not come and collect us on the Friday we were due to spend the weekend with him.

I screamed the whole street down on Friday night.

Hina appeared to have been the cause of Kane not collecting us. She was consumed by her own rage and upset. Hina said to me "he is not coming" in a tone which appeared to be a threat to me that if he came near the house she may kill him. Namaka lay with her arms around Hina for the evening and refused to look at me. Neither of them would acknowledge my tears and screaming. I was in agony. My world had fallen apart and neither of them cared.

From then on, Hina and Namaka made me feel like I was not allowed to want to see Kane. They both appeared to hate him.

I felt alone. A team of one, small, weak and helpless.

I refused to believe Kane was a bad man. I knew he loved me. There were three large bullies in the way. Hina, Namaka, my step mother. None of them seemed to love me. None of them wanted me to see Kane. Each played their part in ensuring I would not.

Then there was another occasion on which I knew Kane was due to collect us, I was very excited. Things were looking up.

However, shortly before he arrived, Hina seemed to be enraged again. I did not know why. She told me we were going out. I protested that we could not go out because Kane was coming to collect us. I ran up the stairs crying, aware that we would be out when Kane arrived.

Namaka chased me angrily up the stairs, on side with Hina's manipulative plot and grabbed me. Namaka was a lot taller and stronger than me at that time. She was seven, I was four. She was angry and violent, I was small and pathetic.

She picked me up, carried me down the stairs whilst I was screaming and crying and put me in the car. The doors were child locked. I had been kidnapped.

We returned, and I did not see Kane.

Kane later told me that more than once he arranged to collect us and Hina ensured we were out. Kane lived a long drive away.

Kane was almost completely absent throughout my childhood, physically and financially. Kane was always in debt. Hina told me she had decided to sell the first family home in order to pay off his debts at that time. He died insolvent though and as far as I can tell, there was never a solvent period in his life. His first conversation with Hina was about horse racing. He loved socialising in bars and pubs. I don't think a day went by where he was without a drink unless he was in hospital.

Hina worked full time. We had two successive nannies. The first of them wore the same black mini dress and thick black patent belt with very high black heels every day (it was the 80's). The next drove a red sports car, ran a dog grooming business and owned an adorably excitable ginger poodle which would leap into my arms to greet me after school. I liked both of them.

I knew Kane loved me, but I was not allowed to see him. I knew there was nothing I could do about this so I got on with school life, which appeared to annoy Namaka. Perhaps because she denied herself the choice to be happy, preferring to seek revenge on the world for inflicting her pain on her. She has said to me in her adult years that she did not understand why I did not appear to be in pain when Kane left. I was, but I knew Kane's love. I carried that with me always and I still do long after he has died. Namaka was always angry and in pain. She took it out on everyone.

The scope for influence on me by Namaka was very wide. I was naïve, I was naturally intrigued by my older and wiser, darker, more experienced sibling. She would act like she knew everything and I knew nothing. Her friends were older than her and male. She was apparently too cool to have a conversation. She had a repertoire of aggressive one line wise cracks.

Her bedroom was mine until one day I found all my belongings moved into the smaller room which used to be hers. A few nights later Hina found me hanging out of the window in my sleep. Fortunately she had heard the wooden curtain rings moving and rescued me before I became a heap of fox fodder on the concrete driveway beneath.

I was always scared of Namaka. It was not only her words which were sharp. She would frequently lose control of her body and become violent in an instant.

Namaka once broke a boy's collar bone in the playground in Primary School. I recall visiting his house with Hina who felt she should apologise (Namaka did not, visit, or feel the need to apologise).

The next occasion Namaka deprived me of a comfort was more disturbing than my security blanket. I had a friend in primary school who bred rabbits. I loved rabbits and persuaded Hina to allow me to have one. I loved my rabbit. I looked after her for a number of years, in a large hutch and run. She was also allowed to run round the garden (supervised of course, and protected from next door's large cat) and one day she mysteriously went missing from her hutch. Namaka behaved very suspiciously and was insistent that I would not find her as she had escaped. This had never happened before and it was not possible. Namaka confessed a number of years later to having killed my rabbit.

The first incidence of violence towards me happened in the kitchen. I was wondering out loud what Namaka was cooking in the boiling pan on the stove. The response from Namaka was to remove the metal slotted spoon from the pan of boiling water together with the egg and put both of them on top of my head. Inevitably I was scolded. Next, she burned one of my eyebrows off: We had made a bonfire in the garden and were standing admiring it. I was standing above the end of one of the branches. Namaka stamped on the other end so that the branch flew up and hit me in the face. It was on fire.

Next, she scarred my forehead: Namaka was once bitten by a Labrador belonging to my uncle. The bite left a scar on her forehead. Namaka scraped her nail down the centre of my forehead so that I too would have a scar. Indeed I do. Namaka was viciously violent towards me. Kicking me, punching me, biting me, pulling my hair. In my teens she threatened me with a heavy metal fire poker with a look in her eyes that said "I will get away with your murder and I will very much enjoy killing you". Namaka is a dark stormy force that I never again want to encounter. She made me believe I caused her to behave that way. That is what abusers do, they make you feel like you deserve it.

Aside from the violence Namaka was continually doing spiteful things to me.

Namaka became a hairdresser as an alternative to doing her A-Levels. I allowed her to "trim an inch" off my long blonde hair which I loved. She trimmed around 8 inches off so it sat above my shoulders. I cried for the rest of the day. I felt naïve and stupid for allowing her near my hair. This incident resonated with me more recently when my long term trusted colourist accidentally blotched my balayage. I had not realized I was still carrying this incident with me.

Hina was depressed at that time and not working, she sat and watched TV all day. I had such a bad argument with her one day that I rang up my friend's father to ask if I could come and stay with them. He very kindly said yes. I didn't speak to Hina for some months. I carried on going to school. I was in my first year of A-Levels at this point.

After a few weeks, Kane organised for me to live with Namaka, paying her money for the rent and food. Namaka lied to me about everything. She was twenty years-old. Her boyfriend lived in the house too. It was such a small house I couldn't do my homework because of the noise of him watching TV when I got home from school. He did not understand the ambition to get good exam results. Shortly before my exams, Namaka came home one day and told me that this arrangement was not working so I had to move out. She said that she had already spoken to a family friend about it and I had to leave immediately and move in there. The family friend was very nice, but she had two sons and a daughter and a small house with no spare room. None of them understood the concept of quiet study.

In that moment, I had what I think was some form of breakdown. I collapsed on the floor with my body in a cramp, violently shaking. I could not mentally digest the idea of possibly failing my exams at the whim of my nasty bitch of a sister.

I wanted to apply to do law and was applying to the best universities. I needed to have grade As in the exams I was about to sit. Everything I had worked towards for the six years up to that point flashed before my eyes and I saw no life at all ahead of me. I would have no education to show for my miserable childhood and no prospect of achieving my potential. The year I applied to university was the last year that grants were available and I assumed I would never be able to go without a grant.

During my breakdown, Namaka rang my step mother, who she (also) hated and never spoke to.

Kane arranged for me to move back to my friend's house.

In that period, I had my Cambridge interview to study law. My interviews went well, but I was "pooled" (put in a group of people who are recommended to other colleges in the university). I realise now that if I had gone I would never had had a relationship with Kane. That was a happy side effect of going to University in London. Everything happens for a reason.

I did not speak to Namaka for some years after that. The next occasion I saw her was her wedding.

Namaka got married aged twenty three, shortly before her twenty fourth birthday. The victim was the man she had been dating, together with a lot of other men, for four years or so.

She gave birth to a son five months later. I assume he was the father, although he is very like Namaka. He was certainly a devoted and loving father. Namaka was a lying cheat. She had one night stands, in remarkably embarrassing circumstances which she relayed to me and other family members in a quest for attention. It is possibly that these were just tales. However, I used to hear Namaka having sex with strange men (one at a time for the most part), in the other bedroom in the house I shared with her. I was once sleeping in my bedroom when I was awoken by a strange man stroking my face. I screamed and told him I would call the police if he didn't leave. He left, confused and slightly panicked. She was having a long term relationship with her future husband at that time.

I had no desire for a relationship with Namaka. I have never had a conversation with her where I have felt that we were just exchanging views about a topic or person and it was honest. Never.

A few months later Namaka gave birth to her son. This occurred on the day of my graduation from university. This upset me because Hina could not wait to leave the ceremony in London to travel to the birth, and Kane cut our trip to a weekend party in Lancashire off to go and meet his new grandson.

I tried to participate more in family events, hoping that Namaka would be a changed person now that she was married with a child. My first conversation involving only the two of us was one in which she told me that she was a different person, in a way which seemed to be apologetic for the things she had done. I said "what do you mean" and she said "I have stopped lying".

Accordingly I made an effort to have a relationship with her. She was always struggling. Her son had heart trouble and she was always in financial difficulty, living in a council house, where she still lives seventeen years later. I did feel sorry for her and I did give her kindness and money. My parents were always worried about her and I was sucked into that too. I believed that is what Kane wanted. After her son was born, Kane tried hard to build a relationship with Namaka. Namaka was still bitter and appeared to always be punishing him. She could not just move on and leave her childhood behind. It was like she wanted to be around him only to remind him that because he abandoned her everything turned out wrong and everything was too hard to bear.

I didn't understand this at all, Kane tried hard and there was an opportunity for a relationship with him.

She bitterly told the family at a party that he had never visited her house. Of course, he had not been invited to at that stage.

At one family party Namaka kicked me violently up the bum because I was dancing with my cousin and we were having fun, which caused her to be consumed by a jealous rage. Later that evening the whole house had to listen to her screaming at her husband for never giving her any attention. This went on for what felt like hours, with calm responses from her husband, for whom I felt desperately sorry. At the same gathering she spewed vicious words at me because I have a law degree. She spewed vicious words at Kane about how difficult marriage was. These were clearly projections of how difficult she had found it to be married and to get an education herself. So I forgave them, so did he.

No one reprimanded her for kicking me. It was abusive and violent, like much of her behaviour towards me and others over the years. There is something about the appearance of her being so consumed by her own pain and anger that makes it impossible to set things right. It is impossible to engage with any particular issue because she appears to have drowned in her own hatred too long ago to acknowledge any of her behaviour as bad. She only knows bad and shocking behaviour.

Everything was an effort for her. She has a masterfully dramatic sigh.

Moving from a seat was an effort. Passing the salt was an effort and would be accompanied by a noise which was something like "ehuckkkkkkkkkkkkkkkkkk". Sitting still was an effort. Everything in her universe was too hard for her to cope with. This makes people feel sorry for her. "She is different", or "She is wired differently", or "She needs extra help".

Namaka wants everyone to believe she is a victim and that she needs their help. She was incapable of listening to anyone else's news and feeling empathy or sympathy for them.

It goes without saying that she was never pleased for me or proud of me, or any of her friends. She talked about her friends in a nasty jealous way.

As I got older, tougher, more professional , more successful and more powerful, her conduct became less obviously violent, and more extreme in other ways. Extreme untruths, extreme spite, made up stories about other members of the family.

Lies about money, lies about her job, lies about her health, lies about what she ate for breakfast, lies about who she slept with, who she drank with, who her friends were, lies about her husband, lies about her in-laws and how they behaved towards her. Everything she said appeared to be a lie. Even if she wasn't lying, nothing made any sense at all so she may as well have been lying. Rational conversations are not in her repertoire, but making up stories and weaving tangled webs of lies are as much a part of her daily life as violent threats.

I realise now I was just another projector for her pain, but the pain she caused me dwelled there for decades. Namaka was vicious. I was too little and fragile to fight back and too nice to believe the things she had actually done. When our relationship struck up again in my twenties, many of them were "confessed" to me like some kind of unburdening of her conscious. I acted like I had moved on from them. I believed that I had. I wanted to believe that she was a new person. But what followed was worse than anything that had gone before.

I only rarely saw Namaka in my twenties. Mainly at family parties. Kane hosted an annual golf tournament in memory of my grandfather, at which the men in the family played golf. It was followed by a family party in the evening with a presentation for the winner and loser. It was always sunny, for which Kane thanked my grandad every year. Kane was a real charmer and everyone loved him (except Namaka apparently), so it was a great success.

Namaka invited a friend to this one year, a school friend of hers. After that evening, Namaka told me various stories about this friend's relationship with my cousin. That they had been seeing each other for a while.

This cousin then met a lovely girl to whom he is ow married. Namaka told tales to me and other family members that her friend was pregnant with my cousin's baby, that she had given birth to the baby and that my cousin was refusing to pay for the baby but maintaining an expensive lifestyle with his new girlfriend. They also included a tale of a visit to my cousin and his girlfriend by the friend and Namaka to introduce my cousin to the baby.

It transpires that the truth of this is that the (Anglo Saxon) friend has a Chinese baby which does not belong to my (Anglo Saxon) cousin.

For some years, Namaka told me and Kane that she had a farm on which she had animals and crops. She also said she was planning to build a house on the land. She maintained that her employer at the time, a large pharmaceutical company, had failed to pay her for the years that she had been working for them and that she received a judgment entitling her to a million pounds in compensation. There is no such judgment and she continued to live in the same council house where she has lived for over two decades.

These lies were puzzling, and appeared to serve no purpose either. They attracted much attention from me and my parents and we wasted a lot of time thinking and talking about them.

Namaka has always made up lies, large and small, and always dramatic.

I received a call from Namaka to tell me that she had a cancerous tumour in her spine but she didn't want any family members to know about it. Naturally I was distressed and shaken up by this news. I wanted to help if at all possible. So I said "of course if there is anything I can do financially to help then please just say". Immediately, Namaka said that she had been told by the hospital that a surgeon would be available to remove the tumour but that she had to travel to Paris to have the operation and it would cost several thousand pounds which she did not have. Of course I didn't hesitate before I told her I would give her the money, and I transferred it to her that day. I did not hear from Namaka on this subject again. Who knows whether she had any operation or what it was. I never saw the money again either.

Kane told me he had to go in to have a heart bypass operation. This came out of the blue as he had not told us he was unwell. I wasn't too worried by this news, he was going into the Hospital and would be operated on by supposedly one of the best surgeons in the country. A few days later I went there to visit him, after his operation. He should have been out of intensive care but he was still lying unconscious on a drip. That was hard to deal with. The surgeon told me he was meant to have stopped bleeding but he was still losing a huge volume of blood. They could not say why and so they would be opening up his chest again to try to establish the cause. Ka was next to arrive. I was crying, upset that Kane was unconscious on a drip and no one could say when he would be conscious again. Ka was upset at the sight of me, and more upset when he saw Kane.

It was about a week before Kane was conscious again. I arrived at the hospital the day he was conscious again and just cried on his wounded chest. It was half term for Ka. He spent it in the hospital. He did not get along well with Namaka, who was also there. Namaka was chirpy and would not stop talking. It was just noise, seemingly so all of our attention would be on Namaka. I found it insensitive and irritating. Kane needed rest. I asked him if he had eaten dinner. He said "yes love, I've had a carrot, and an onion". I looked at the hospital dinner menu, it had a picture of a carrot and an onion." Kane was conscious, but clearly not with us.

It transpired that he had suffered a stroke during his operation. He was in the hospital for a few weeks recovering very slowly.

Hi-iaka was financially reliant on Kane, who was in mountains of debt. I don't know if she knew that and did not care, or if Kane deliberately kept this from her and wanted the large expensive wedding for her in order to impress his friends. He was to be paying for a wedding for her in any case. It seems that this wedding was the bulk of the debt Kane owed when he later died insolvent.

I helped Hi-iaka with the wedding, I wanted her to have a fantastic day. I took her shopping for her bridesmaids dresses and paid for them. I paid for fireworks, which had been choreographed to her favourite songs. I had earlier that year paid for a group of her friends to go to Ascot in the Royal enclosure for her hen do. I bought a horse from her to financially assist them, and her in laws, who would be paid to train the horse.

Hi-iaka has three adorable children now and a very happy family.

Kane was often in financial distress. He spent very little money himself. He gave away all the capital in his family house in his second divorce. I wanted to please him, and I hated to see him stressed so I helped him a lot. He wanted Ka and Hi-iaka to see him as "their rock". He did not recognise that he put a lot of strain on me. He said to me "You are the only one of my children I do not worry about". This hurt me sometimes. I felt that he worried about the others because he cared. I did not tell him my worries because I felt that he did not care for me. I felt I had to get his attention by being a joy to be around, being kind and helpful. The rest of the family just appeared to ask him for help and he would ask me to help them.

Namaka sent us all a very offensive text message whilst Kane was in hospital and she was getting on with life elsewhere.

When Kane was conscious again, she made sure he was aware that she attended the hospital when he was not. He was conscious in the hospital for several weeks, so he may have assumed she had not visited at all. She also remarked that she would not want to be cut from his will because he wouldn't remember that she visited him in hospital. I did not understand this remark, Kane was in so much debt he did not have an "estate".

A short time later, Namaka extracted three thousand pounds from me under the false pretence that she needed it for a few days whilst money went from one of her accounts to another. She kept on texting me reasons why the money had not been paid back. It rapidly became apparent that her texts were lies. This was very time consuming and draining.

I did not speak to her for the rest of the year, nor did I get my money back. The next time we spoke Namaka rang me in hysterical tears because Kane was in hospital with the stroke that would kill him a week later. The hysterics were in order to get me to communicate with her and forget the fraud of earlier that year in favour of being united in the face of a devasting crisis. Again, she would make me feel naïve, stupid and manipulated. Whilst me, Ka and Hi-iaka were experiencing grief and devastation, Namaka would start a storm to batter us in our vulnerable state.

When Kane died that year, Namaka wreaked havoc with the funeral plans, caused arguments all over the family and orchestrated a fraud on the creditors of his estate by writing herself a cheque which she told the bank and us that Kane had written her before he died "in case anything happened" in order that she would be able to pay for his funeral. I obtained the cheque from the bank a year later. It was in Namaka's handwriting.

This lie was surrounded by a complex web of other lies and upset. Namaka said that the cheque was accompanied by a letter from Kane which she did not want any of us to see because it contained some difficult truths about Kane that Hi-iaka and Ka should be sheltered from. We were grieving the death of Kane and Namaka was abusing us.

Namaka tried to bankrupt Ka, luring him into agreeing to pay the funeral caterers on the understanding that Namaka would pay them out of the said cheque. Namaka instead spent the cheque for her own purposes. Not only did Namaka not pay the caterers, but she made up a number of different lies to me and Ka so that I did not pay them for him. After several months of more and more extreme lies from Namaka about the payment of the caterer, Ka received a formal bankruptcy threat. I paid the caterer at that point.

Namaka and I no longer speak. I feel empowered by the decision I made to cut her out of my life. It took me years of abuse and lies for which she made me feel responsible before I finally cut the chord. Every conversation with her or about her was exhausting.

Her husband died shortly after that, mysteriously and at the age of fourty two. I had been very fond of him. I went to his funeral. I gave her my condolences that her husband had died. She gave me no apology for the web of lies she wove when Kane died. There was no acknowledgement of the pain she had inflicted.

"Life is short" she said, "we must get together". All that I thought in that moment was "I don't think we do need to get together. However long my life on earth will be, I consider it too short to waste energy on you."

I found that writing all of these events down and how I felt about them at the time made me recognize the emotions which seem real to me but are actually me living in the past.

It takes complete awareness and practice to acknowledge the emotions we experience in any given moment. This is the key to releasing the past.

"I love all my relationships"	
PAST	**NOW AND FOREVER**
	I feel loved
	I feel safe
	I feel strong
	I feel empowered
	I am happy
	I am joyful
	I laugh often

9 LET IT SHINE

Luckily for me, I failed in my darkest effort. Years on and with Pele's work, I do not believe I am the same person who tried to kill myself. I discovered how to take responsibility for my own happiness.

I can't and I don't want to imagine ever feeling like trying to take my own life again. I choose to be excited every day about the fact I am alive. I am grateful for my every moment of my life. I am living it, and I am loving it. Feeling suicidal is something in my life that I draw great strength from because it made me focus on what I want. It was a point in my life where I could not feel any worse, my rock bottom. The only place to look from there is up. I have been climbing ever since. That is not an expression of social mobility, nor indeed is it a measure of my achievements. It is a measure of my self-love.

If you don't feel the love, call on Pele.

ABOUT THE AUTHOR

The author struggled with anxiety illnesses for two decades and tried to kill herself.
This is her journey to power.

30434429R00039

Printed in Great Britain
by Amazon